W9-AUG-145

GROWING UP

IN, WITH, AND UNDER JESUS

PETER BERAUER

CONTENTS

INTRODUCTION

This is a book about Christian maturity.

I have been blessed with many mature Christian role models. One of them was a man named Ed. Before he died, Ed lived in a small, 10x10 room at a nearby nursing home. I would go to visit Ed from time to time to pray, read Scripture, and celebrate the Lord's Supper. I always looked forward to visiting Ed.

The only problem was that Ed didn't know who I was. He probably didn't even know who he was, where he was, or why I was coming to visit him. Ed had dementia, and his words were few and far between.

We couldn't have a conversation. I never got to hear about his wife, kids, or career. He never told me a story or laughed at my jokes. But, in so many ways, I looked up to Ed.

That's because there came a moment in each of our visits when it would be time to pray.

"Let's pray, Ed," I would say. And, somehow, words would pour out of this quiet man.

"Our Father, who art in heaven . . . ," Ed would say.

Later, we would read some Scripture, and Ed's eyes would light up. Here and there he would finish a sentence from a verse he recognized. When it came time for Communion, while holding up the wafer and a little cup of wine, I would ask, "Ed, do you know what this is?"

"Jesus," Ed would say. And then He would open his mouth wide, the edges of his lips curling up, his eyes focused on that wafer. Ed was ready to receive his Savior.

You see, Ed had spent his life growing up in, with, and under Jesus. He had read the Scriptures, gone to church, prayed, served, and shared his faith throughout his years. God had filled him up over decades with Jesus. And now, in his last days, it was like he was overflowing with Christ. Everything else had been taken from Ed by the time I met him: his wife, his home, his memories, and his mind. Ed's life looked empty, but he was really full. Ed had been filled with Jesus. Even though I hadn't known him during his formative years in the faith, it was clear that

Ed had spent a lifetime growing up in, with, and under Jesus.

I want to be like Ed.

—————

We all need mature Christian role models. Not only do they reflect Christ's love in real, tangible ways, but they also paint us a picture of what it looks like to live as a Christian in this world. They show us what it looks like to be God's Son or Daughter in this messy world we all live in.

I hope and pray that you have mature Christians in your life that you can look up to, that motivate and inspire you, and that show you what it looks like to follow Jesus. And in some small way, that's what this book is about as well. Nothing can replace the Christian witness of real people living out the faith, but I pray that in these pages you will see a picture of what it means to mature in your faith and what it looks like to grow up in, with, and under Jesus.

—————

"I don't have to go to church every week to be a Christian! I can pray and read my Bible at home."

"God still loves me even if I don't [give money to the church, go to Bible study, volunteer, etc.]."

"God knows what I'm thinking and what I need—so why should I bother praying?"

"It's not that big of a deal. And after all, God will forgive me if I [lie, gossip, lust, etc.]."

"The people at church are old and boring. I can be a Christian without joining a church, and I'll definitely have more fun doing something else!"

As a pastor, I have heard a lot of people say something like the above statements. If I'm candid, I've used a few of those lines too. And, quite honestly, all of them are true! You don't have to go to church every week to be a Christian. God will forgive you if you gossip or lie. He will love you even if you don't put money in the offering plate. He does know what you are thinking and what you need even if you don't tell Him. And, most of us could find something more "fun" to be doing on Sunday mornings than going to church.

While true, these attitudes don't reflect Christian maturity. The mature Christians I have met simply don't say, or think, things like that. Instead of making excuses for skipping church, they look for ways to be more faithful in attendance. Instead of dismissing their sin, they repent of it, ask for forgiveness, and try to do better. The mature Christians I have gotten to know pray and serve in local churches even though it's not glamorous, fun, or exciting. The mature Christians I look up to don't look for ways to avoid Christian practices, and they don't seek to perform the minimum requirement or effort. They simply trust in Jesus and strive to do their best to reflect Him in their lives. I want to be like them.

All of us have growing up to do. I wish I could say that I am writing this book because I am one of those fully mature Christians and am now able to share my vast knowledge with younger, less mature Christians. I wish that Christian maturity was a reality I have reached or a finish line I have crossed. But, that couldn't be further from the truth.

Instead, I am writing this book because it is one I need to read. The words you are reading on this page are words that I need to be written on my heart. These words are written to myself as much as to anyone else.

The truth is that none of us reaches full Christian maturity this side of Heaven. The moment we think we have attained perfection is probably the moment that we are farthest away from it.

Which doesn't mean that we shouldn't strive toward maturity. In fact, God commands spiritual maturity and growth. In 1 Corinthians 14:20, He says through Paul, "Brothers and sisters, don't be childish in your thinking." God loves children. Jesus welcomed them, even when the disciples wanted to keep them away. He accepts people who have nothing to offer Him. In one sense, we are all God's children. But, He doesn't want us to remain children when we are able to mature. He wants us to keep working toward a more Christ-like life and faith. He wants us to grow up.

This is how Paul puts it in Ephesians 4:14-15, "Then we will no longer be little children, tossed by the waves and blown around by every wind of teaching, by human cunning with cleverness in the techniques of deceit. But, speaking the truth in love, let us grow in every way into him who is the head—Christ." The Christian life was designed to be one of continual growth.

I understand that a lot of this book might seem like

Law (God's guidelines, commands, and rules for our lives) rather than Gospel (what Christ has done for us). That's because most of it is. At the end of each chapter you will find practices, habits, and disciplines you can follow. While these are meant to be suggestions, and many are habits I have found to be helpful, they are not the Gospel. Many of the pages will describe how you can reflect Christ in your thinking, desiring, speaking, and acting. While my intention was not to write a spiritual how-to manual, my hope is that these practices will spur on Christian living among God's people.

So while a lot of the book will be Law, let's remember that God's Law is good! The Law shows us how to think, desire, speak, and act. When we've sinned, it works like a mirror, showing us our need for Jesus. It keeps us on track when we are tempted to do the wrong thing. All of that is good . . . unless we put our faith wholly in that Law. We were never meant to trust in God's Law or our ability to keep it. Instead, the Law is there to point us to Jesus. It forces us to see how much we need Him, and then guides us to live more like Him.

I decided to call this book *Growing Up In, With, and Under Jesus* because that's what Christian maturity is: growth. It is also a life *in* Jesus: clothed in Him in Baptism and wrapped in His grace. It is a life *with* Jesus: walking with Him all our days as He leads us. It's a life *under* Jesus: under His Lordship and under the banner of His grace.

Which brings me to one last important note: While we grow in, with, and under Jesus, we never grow *out* of Jesus. As we grow and mature, we never stop needing our Savior. Quite the opposite. The more we grow up, the more we recognize our need for Him.

Which is how it always is, isn't it? That's definitely how it is with our parents when we are young. As we grow and mature, over time we start acting different. Through the years we slowly start thinking, desiring, speaking, and acting like mom and dad. We mature. But, over that same period of time we also recognize how much we need them. No mature child ever says, "Now that I'm mature I realize how little I need my parents. What a waste all those years were! I could have taken care of myself!" I know that the older I get, the more thankful I am for all that my parents have done. I see more clearly all the ways I fell short as their child, and more than ever I know that I still need them.

And that's how it is with God. Over time we will

start thinking, desiring, speaking, and acting more like Jesus. But, we will never outgrow Him. We will always need Him. And over time we will see Him prove Himself faithful over and over again.

That is what it looks like to grow up in, with, and under Jesus.

CHAPTER 1

GROWING UP IN, WITH, AND UNDER: GOD'S WORD

As Christians, we absorb God's Word as often as possible.

My grandmother was full of stories. Stories that I loved to hear. Whenever she came over to watch us, I remember asking her to tell me another story. I couldn't get enough.

Most of her stories were about her life during WWII. My grandmother grew up in Eastern Europe, in a town that various governments fought for control of. She had stories of fighter jets that dropped bombs on her sleepy town. Stories of all the men in the village being paraded in the streets before being shot dead.

Stories of hidden compartments in the furniture where her family could hide valuables from the soldiers who searched their homes.

The stories that really gripped me were the stories of the time she spent in work-camps. Toward the end of the war, one of the battling governments' armies took her and many other women from her town to camps where they were forced to provide free labor. Looking back on it now, these stories were grizzly. Her experiences were terrifying. I don't know how she relived them for me.

Through all those stories I learned a lot about my grandmother. Now that she's gone I treasure those stories. The stories told me more than just the facts of her life. They also told me who she was on a much deeper level. They revealed her strength, her compassion, and her determination.

But, that's not all I learned from those stories. I didn't know it at the time, but now I see that I was also learning my story. I was learning who I was: where I came from, what made me who I am, and how I got to be where I am today. My grandmother's story is also my own.

God's Word, as we hear it in the Bible, is one big story. Sometimes we think about the Bible as a book of rules (and there are rules in the Bible). Other times we value it for its wisdom (and the Bible is full of godly wisdom). Or maybe we think of it as a book of spiritual guidelines with helpful hints for godly living (there is a lot of that too). But, the Christian Scriptures are primarily a story: God's story.

The Bible starts with the story of how God created the world and how He formed Adam and Eve out of nothing. It's the story of how, despite their constant sin and rebellion, God pursued and chased after His people with love. It's a story about His promise of a Savior and His plan to keep that promise and see it through. It's the story of the Son He sent, the cross He died on, and the promise He made to return one day. The Scriptures are the story of God's Church, which He holds onto tightly and guides securely by His Spirit.

The Scriptures are a story that find its culmination and fulfillment in Jesus. That's what Jesus tells us himself. Early in John's Gospel, in chapter 5, Jesus has just healed a man on the Sabbath day. The Sabbath was a day that was given to God's people as a gift. It was a day to rest and receive, rather than to do and give. For Jesus to work a miracle on the Sabbath went against everything the religious leaders thought the Sabbath was about.

That's because these religious leaders had read the Scriptures as a book full of rules and laws (just like many people do today). They thought that if they could just keep all those rules they would find true life. They didn't see that all of the Bible was a story pointing to Jesus, and that in Jesus you find true life. These religious people had turned God's gift (in this case, the Sabbath) into a burden. And so Jesus needed to teach them that if you don't see Jesus everywhere you look in the Scriptures, you are missing out.

Jesus told them, "You pore over the Scriptures because you think you have eternal life in them, and yet they testify about me." The day of rest and receiving called the Sabbath was always there to point God's people to the eternal Sabbath rest that is found not in a day, but in the person of Jesus Christ. These religious leaders needed to know that the Scriptures were a story and what that story was all about.

Later in Jesus' life, He teaches this same lesson to His own disciples. Three days after Jesus died on the cross, He rose again. It was a miracle so amazing His own followers had a hard time believing it. Two of them were walking along the road one day, still in disbelief over all that had just happened, when Jesus came up to them. The three of them started talking, and eventually Jesus began to show them that these events shouldn't have been a surprise. After all, the Scriptures had promised them. Luke writes in his Gospel, "Then beginning with Moses and all the Prophets, he (Jesus) interpreted for them all the things concerning himself in all the Scriptures." Jesus had to show them that the whole story was all about Him.

The Bible is God's story, but it's also our story too. It's the story of Jesus for us. When we read about the fall of Adam and Eve, we are reading about our first parents. Through their story we learn how we got to where we are today. Through the stories of evil kings and wicked rulers, but also faithful women and Spirit-filled prophets, we learn our family history. We hear how God sent Jesus to live for us and die for us and rise for us.

What an amazing story. And the greatest part is that it's true! The Bible isn't just a collection of fairy-tales with a message. It's not just a series of moral lessons or fables that are meant to point us toward a life of greater meaning. Neither is it a series of metaphors leading us toward a spiritual truth. The Bible is the true Word of God given to His people.

God's Word has two primary messages to speak to us: Law and Gospel. The overarching message of the story is that we are sinners with an amazing Savior.

God's Law is His will for our life. It tells us what to do (Honor your Father and Mother) and what not to do (You shall not steal). God's will for our lives goes deeper than actions though. God's will penetrates our thoughts, desires, and beliefs.

Whenever we hear God's message of Law, God works through it in any combination of three ways. First, God's Law convicts us. When we hear it, we are reminded of our sin and our need for a Savior. Second, it keeps us on track. Whenever we think about stealing or lying, it's the Law that reminds us that these things have no part to play in the life of a Christian. Finally, the Law teaches us how to live. Much of God's will doesn't come to us naturally. We need to learn it. Left on my own, I might think it is a pretty good idea to live selfishly and materialistically. It's God's message of Law that shows us God's way.

The Law is good, but it has its limitations. The

Law demands perfection, but it can't give it. The Law can't give us what we desperately need: forgiveness and grace. Thank God that it's not the only message God has spoken to us.

The other message we hear in God's Word is the Gospel. The Gospel is the Good News of Jesus' life, death, and resurrection. It is about what God has done for us, not about what we do for Him. The Gospel is a gift of love that can't be earned or deserved. The Gospel message is the overarching message that gives all of God's Word its shape. It's our hope, our life, and our rest.

Both the Law and the Gospel are good for us. But, they have very different purposes. The Law kills. The Gospel brings life. The Law says, "Do this." The Gospel says, "Jesus already did it all." We need the Law and the Gospel. Without the Law, we wouldn't know God's will and would be content in our sin. We wouldn't know how much we need a savior. Without the Gospel, we would be dead in our sins and trespasses. Life would be hopeless.

It's the dual message of Law and Gospel that comes through to us in the story of the Scriptures that we need to constantly hear: we are sinners with a Savior.

When I was in college, I had a professor who had memorized the entire Bible. My fellow students and I were amazed at this. We often turned it into a game, calling out Bible verses and asking him to recite them. Most of us had no idea how to comprehend how this was possible. We had all struggled to memorize a single verse here and there, but this man had absorbed the entirety of Scripture into his mind!

One day at his on-campus apartment over dinner, the quizzing continued. He kindly played along for a little, reciting obscure verses, barely pausing to think. After a while, one of us asked how he was able to do this. I still remember his answer all these years later: "I love God's Word," he said. "And I spend as much time in it as possible."

I thought for a time after that conversation that I would be like my professor and memorize my Bible. I won't even tell you how long that lasted. But, what has stuck with me are his words, "I love God's Word. And I spend as much time in it as possible." That's Christian maturity. That's something to strive for. That's something to grow up into.

In the Bible we read God's written Word. The Bible gives us surety and assurances of what God has said. It provides a steady, Holy Spirit—inspired, unchanging foundation for everything we believe to be good and true. We can count on it because it's not just a collection of nice thoughts and ideas. 2 Timothy 3:16 tells us that "All Scripture is inspired by God." And 2 Peter 1:21 reminds us that "No prophecy ever came by the will of man; instead, men spoke from God as they were carried along by the Holy Spirit." What an amazing gift the Bible is to us!

Mature Christians spend as much time in the Bible as possible. We read it on our own, to our families, with our friends, and at church. We memorize verses from it, listen to it on our phones, and mark up our Bibles with our reflections and questions. As mature Christians, we let the Bible's words shape and mold us.

But, God's Word also comes to us in other ways. Sometimes we sing God's Word in songs and hymns. Other times we hear it preached to us in sermons or spoken to us by friends who remind us that "God loves you!"

And, as Christians, we thank God for His Word whenever it comes to us, in whatever way that might be. Just because we went to worship on Sunday and heard the Word doesn't mean that we don't need a

Tuesday night Bible study. Or, just because we can read our Bible at home by ourselves doesn't mean we don't need the Sunday morning sermon. Mature Christians look to absorb as much of God's Word as possible. We dig down, dive in, and deepen our study because of how precious it is to us. God's Word is one we love, and need, to hear. We listen because it's both God's story and our own. We listen as it proclaims to us the ever-needful messages of Law and Gospel. We listen, because we need to hear about Jesus.

Growing in God's Word draws us further in, with, and under the love and grace of Jesus.

HEALTHY HABITS FOR MATURE CHRISTIANS: GOD'S WORD

1. Read one chapter of the Bible each day. As you read, ask yourself: (1) What questions do I have? (2) What stands out, or what is something new I've noticed? (3) What comfort is given in Christ? (4) How am I challenged to think, talk, or act differently? (5) What sins am I led to confess?

2. Attend a Bible study through your church to learn more about God's Word.

3. Memorize one Bible verse a week so that God's Word dwells within you.

4. Attend worship to sing, hear, speak, and read God's Word with your family in Christ.

5.Read a devotional book written by a Christian with reflections on Scripture. Ask your pastor or a Christian friend for recommendations.

CHAPTER 2

GROWING UP IN, WITH, AND UNDER: PRAYER

As Christians, we continually pray to a loving God who hears us.

Your God loves to hear from you, and He invites you to talk to Him in prayer. After all, God calls us to "Pray constantly" (1 Thessalonians 5:17). Prayer is nothing but speaking to God in response to His speaking to us in His Word. Prayer is the words of God's people lifted up to the God who promises to listen.

It tells us a lot about God that when Jesus taught His disciples to pray what we know as the Lord's Prayer He began His prayer with the words "Our Father." God lovingly invites us to talk to Him like kids talk with mom and dad. He wants to hear our complaints and groaning. He invites our words of grief and sadness. He welcomes our calls and cries of confusion and questioning. He listens as we praise Him and thank Him for all He's done.

God intently pays attention as you ask your questions and make your requests. He is your Father, and He loves to hear from you, His child.

When God hears our voices, He listens. He always answers when we call. He never tires of opening His ears to our words.

▭

Several years ago I was helping out at our church's Vacation Bible School (VBS). For one week I was in charge of showing a five-minute video clip to the children attending VBS, and then passing out the snack of the day. To be honest, as a soon-to-be pastor I thought the job I had been assigned was a little beneath me. I thought I should be leading a deep theological discussion on the Trinity, not passing out goldfish crackers and vanilla cookies.

But, on the very first day, I learned an important lesson on prayer from a sister in Christ who was much more mature than I was. I had shown the video clip, passed out the snack, and told the kids to hurry up and eat. That's when one little girl, maybe four years old, quietly and kindly raised her hand. I thought maybe she had been skipped over and wanted a cup of Kool-Aid.

"Shouldn't we pray first?" she asked. "I think we should talk to God before we eat," she humbly told her know-it-all teacher.

You see, she got it. She understood that God invites us to talk to him all of the time: not just before a big test or scary operation, but also before a meal of crackers and fruit punch. This little four-year-old girl understood that her Heavenly Father loves to hear from His children. She wanted to talk to Him. And not out of guilt or obligation, or because she wanted to check off a box on her spiritual to-do list. No, she wanted to pray because she knew she had a God who listened, who cared, and who loved her. Who wouldn't want to talk to a God like that?

I've heard it said that "There's no wrong way to pray." That sounds nice, but I'm not sure that it's exactly true. Jesus seems to suggest that there is a wrong way. He talks about it in Matthew chapter 6. "Whenever you pray, you must not be like the hypocrites, because they love to pray standing in the synagogues and on the street corners to be seen by people. Truly I tell you, they have their reward. But when you pray, go into your private room, shut your door, and pray to your Father who is in secret" (Matthew 6:5-6).

Jesus makes it clear that we are not to pray like the hypocrites of His day, who loved to pray out in public in order to be seen by other people. Prayer is not about being recognized, noticed, and applauded by other people. It's also not about earning God's approval or love. We don't pray just to check a box off our list or to pat ourselves on the back for being so "spiritual."

Just as much as prayer is words, it's also a posture. I don't mean that in order to pray we need to fold our hands neatly or get down on our knees. Prayer is an inner posture of humility toward God. It is bowing down before Him to say, "I can't, but you can!" It is a posture of neediness that says, "Lord, you have things for me that I can't get on my own." It is a recognition that there are limitations to our abilities, and boundaries to our capacities. We need God, and by the simple act of praying we recognize that need.

Prayer is a conversation with the God who notices us no matter the eloquence or length of our prayers.That's not to say that some days our prayers won't be long. Sometimes we have lots to pray about: lots to thank Him for, lots of praises to give, lots of concerns and worries, and lots of needs that only He can provide.

And some days our prayers might even be eloquent. We might surprise ourselves when the words just flow. Praise God for those times! But, God even hears the stumbling prayers of a child who cries out, "Daddy, help me!" or "Lord, have mercy!" or "I believe! Help my unbelief!"

———

To be sure, God hears our short, stumbling, last-second prayers. He listens when we feel like we have no words. When we sit in the hospital room of someone we love with nothing to say but, "Help me, Lord!" God hears. When we find ourselves hitting the brakes to avoid a crash while driving and calling out, "Dear God, please!" God listens. It is good to call out to God wherever we are, whatever we are doing, whenever we need Him.

But, it is also good to approach prayer with intentionality. Maturity doesn't say, "God knows me and my needs even if I don't pray." Of course God knows what we need before we say it. That doesn't mean we don't bring everything to Him anyway. It was the same when we were kids. More often than not, our parents knew we were hungry before we told them. They could see the sadness in our eyes before we came to them in tears. Our parents could tell when we had gotten into a fight at school before we ever said a word. But, that didn't mean they didn't want to have the conversation. Of course they did! Even though they could tell what was going on, they still wanted to engage. It's the same way with God.

Maturity says, "I can't wait to tell my Father what happened today," and "I need to stop carrying around this burden and instead give it over to the one who can bear it," or "I just want to say thank you for all my God has given me!"

And so, it's good for us to set aside some time to pray each day and to form patterns or habits of prayer. Just because God knows what we need before we do doesn't mean we don't want to intentionally bring Him our needs and requests. And so we write out our prayers to make sure we cover everything we need. We learn and memorize the prayers of the Church to learn from brothers and sisters in Christ who give us the words when we have none. We find quiet places where the distractions are minimal so that we can devote our time to the Lord. We keep lists so that we remember who we said we would pray for and to keep track of answered prayers. God's invitation to talk to Him in prayer is an amazing gift, one that Christians take advantage of as often as possible. A healthy prayer life helps us grow up in, with, and under Jesus.

HEALTHY HABITS FOR MATURE CHRISTIANS: PRAYER

1. Pray the Lord's Prayer each day.

2. Memorize another pre-written prayer (for example, "Luther's Morning Prayer"). Prayers that other mature Christians have written and prayed can help you to grow in your own personal prayer life.

3. Pray one of the psalms each day. When you have no words to pray, let God's Word guide you.

4. Write out your prayer following the ACTS model (Adorations, Confessions, Thanksgivings, Supplications/requests). Consider starting a prayer journal where you write out your prayers each day. Over time

you will see how God has answered your prayers and how He has worked in your life.

5.Find a prayer partner to pray with. Share requests and thanksgivings with one another. You could even do this over email or text.

CHAPTER 3

GROWING UP IN, WITH, AND UNDER: THE CHURCH AND WORSHIP

As Christians, we are part of a great big family called the Church, and together as brothers and sisters God pours out gifts to us in worship.

In the book of Genesis we hear the story of Jacob and Leah. Jacob and Leah were husband and wife, but it was a marriage and a lifelong bond that Jacob did not choose.

As the story goes, Jacob first falls in love with Leah's sister, Rachel. It's almost love at first sight. From their first meeting on, Jacob is determined to marry Rachel. He even agrees to work seven years for

Rachel's father Laban in order to take her home as his wife.

At the end of the seven years the time has finally come. On the wedding night Laban pulls a pretty sinister trick. When the party is over, he sends Leah in to sleep with Jacob. Because of the veil she was probably wearing and the darkness of the night, Jacob is fooled. The marriage is consummated, but now he's married to the wrong girl!

Over time Jacob will need to learn to love the wife he didn't choose. This wasn't part of Jacob's plan. Leah wasn't the woman he would have picked. But, they are joined together now, and Jacob has to figure out how to love the person God has placed him with.

———

Hear me out now—that is sort of what it is like to be a part of God's Church. While God talks about the Church in many different ways—as a Body, as a Kingdom full of citizens—my favorite way to think about it is as a family. The Church is full of brothers and sisters, as the Apostle Paul reminds us throughout his letters. Every believer in Jesus is a part of this family: The Church.

And just like Jacob, we are joined to men and

women we didn't choose. They might not be our first love. They might not be the kind of people we would choose to spend the weekend with. But, we are called to love these people. They are our brothers and sisters. And despite what we might think, God is probably working through them to teach, serve, and show us things we need to learn and receive. These people become Jesus to us. I don't mean that they are the ones that died on the cross for us, but that Christ shows His love to us through them in real, tangible ways.

Many of the people that I've been in churches with are not people I would naturally gravitate toward. Most weren't my age, many didn't cheer for my sports teams, and much of the time we didn't have much in common. But, these faithful men and women have showed me things that I otherwise wouldn't have seen. I need these people God has put me with.

One brother that I think about is Ray. Ray was not a man I would have normally befriended. He was quite a bit older than me, we came from different backgrounds, and had little to talk about. If we had met each other at a bar, we would have struggled to keep a conversation going. But, Ray showed me a lot about what it means to be a part of God's family. It wasn't that Ray wowed me with his deep spiritual knowledge. It wasn't that his prayers were eloquent and wise. No, Ray showed me what it looks like to love the Church, God's family.

Despite being elderly, Ray was always the one to snow-blow the church's sidewalks in winter. He would stay late into the night or wake up early to make sure that the rest of us could get into church safely.

The first winter I met Ray there was a terrible, record-setting snowstorm that blasted our area. At the time, I lived in the church's parsonage, a home on church property that the congregation provided to me for my ministry there. Just before the storm came, I had moved my car into a place I thought would keep it safe from the wind and snow. But, the narrow alleyway I left it in ended up acting like a wind-tunnel that completely covered my car.

As a young, twenty-something man, I thought this would be no problem. But, I spent hours trying to free my car from the snow with little luck. The snow was falling faster than I could shovel, and pretty soon I realized it was going to take me days to get my car out of the snow. I went to bed that night wondering if I was going to have to wait until spring for the snow to melt before I could drive again.

The next morning I could barely believe what I

saw when I looked out the window to that alley. I woke up to a clean driveway and a car that had been set free! Ray had spent hours shoveling and snow-blowing. No one had asked him to do that. It certainly wasn't because I was worthy or because he was returning a favor. Ray just loved the church, his family. And so, Ray served. He sacrificed. All for a brother Christian he barely knew.

Mature Christians recognize that they are part of a family. They take on certain responsibilities, not because they are fun or even because they feel "passionately" about that particular cause. Instead, mature Christians like Ray sacrifice and serve out of love for their brothers and sisters. And through mature Christians like Ray the rest of us see glimpses of the love of Jesus.

All of us need people like Ray. We need brothers and sisters in the faith. We might not think we do. We might like to think that we are capable all on our own to walk this life of faith. We have Jesus after all, and isn't that all we need? But, God knew that none of us could go it alone. He has surrounded us with brothers and sisters. He brought us into His family. None of us is an only child. Our family is there to surround us with joy when we are sad, encouragement when we are down, strength when we are weak, and to put us in our place when we've started to wander.

God reminds us of this in Romans chapter 12. He talks about the Church being a Body, one Body, but with many parts. God makes it clear that every part of the Body is crucial. "As it is, there are many parts, but one body. The eye cannot say to the hand, 'I don't need you!' Or again, the head can't say to the feet, 'I don't need you!' On the contrary, those parts of the body that are weaker are indispensable" (1 Corinthians 12:20-22).

Mature Christians become active parts of the Body of Christ. We find ways to love our brothers and sisters in Jesus. We serve, sacrifice, and encourage the people God has surrounded us with. Mature Christians see the value of the local church—not as an institution, but as a family God has brought us into. And so, mature Christians give up their time, talents, and treasures to support the family He has given us. We need these brothers and sisters, and they need us! By not actively engaging in a local church, not only are we missing out, but others are missing out on what we bring to the family. Being a part of the Church is both an amazing gift and a responsibility to be taken seriously.

Jesus unconditionally loved His Church family so much that He went to the cross to die for it. As His people, we unconditionally love and sacrifice for the good for the family too.

━━

Each week, for centuries, God's family has gathered together for a weekly reunion called worship. Worship is the time when we come together to sit at our Father's feet as He pours out gifts to us. It might be the one time during our busy weeks that we hear Him speak as we listen attentively. Worship re-orientates us to God's ways. We've spent the previous six days listening to the ways of the world, but in worship we hear about God's ways, about His great love, and about what life looks like as His children. Worship is not primarily an obligation demanded by an angry God that we have to fulfill. Worship is not just a box we need to check on the to-do list of being spiritual. Worship is a gift from God to His people—a gift we desperately need!

And so, we go to worship each week because we receive things there that we need. We hear God's Word spoken from the Scriptures, sung in our songs, and recited in the Creed. We are reminded of His promises to us and who we are as His baptized children. We receive His Body and Blood for the forgiveness of our sins. In worship God pours out grace upon grace and we come face to face with Jesus.

A lot of us think about worship as something that we do. And, it is that, of course. We do respond to God's amazing love and faithfulness with songs of praise and adoration. We do pray to Him and thank Him for all He's done. But, it starts with Him. He makes the first move. God takes the first step in worship. And He's bringing us exactly what we need. Mature Christians joyfully come to worship because they recognize how much they need it.

Maturity also recognizes that in worship, we are surrounded by a family who needs us too. As much as we need what God is giving us, there are brothers and sisters in the seats around us who need us there. They need our encouragement. They need our strength. They need our presence as a witness to God's presence among us. Even as you sit in your pew, thinking no one would notice if you weren't there, you are representing the presence of Jesus to the people around you.

God reminds us of this in Hebrews chapter 10. There we hear, "And let us watch out for one another to provoke love and good works, not neglecting to gather together as some are in the habit of doing, but encouraging each other and all the more as you see the day approaching." Like any family, we need each other. By not showing up to worship, not only are you missing out on what the people in the pew have to give you, but they are missing out on what you have to offer them.

———

Most of what we hear and receive in worship is not isolated to within the four walls of a church building or to an hour on Sunday morning. Of course we can read God's Word at home. We can, and should, pray wherever and whenever we can. We can sing God's praises in our cars and showers.

But, Christian maturity doesn't say, "I don't need to go to church. I can do most of that at home!" Maturity says, "If God is ready and willing to pour out the most amazing gifts of love and grace to me, who am I to say no?" Maturity doesn't say, "How often do I have to go to church?" Maturity says, "How can I get there as often as I can?" Maturity recognizes that we are not in a position to turn down such an amazing opportunity to gather together with brothers and sisters around our gracious God.

Mature Christians thank God for His family, the Church. They look for ways to get actively involved in the family business. They joyfully and regularly attend worship to receive God's gifts, reflect His presence, and to be challenged and encouraged by the rest of the family. Through the Church and worship God's people grow up in, with, and under Jesus.

HEALTHY HABITS FOR MATURE CHRISTIANS: THE CHURCH AND WORSHIP

1. Regularly attend worship.

2.Recite the Apostles' or Nicene Creed each day as a reminder that Christians throughout the world and history share your faith in Jesus.

3.Offer to drive an elderly member to worship.

4.Grab coffee or lunch with a member at your church you don't know well. Get to know them as a brother or sister in Christ. Pray for them.

5.Financially contribute to your local congregation. Work toward "tithing" or giving 10 percent of your income as God's people have done since Moses' time. You won't just be funding a dying institution or getting God off your back. You'll be supporting the Gospel and God's work to continue in that place.

CHAPTER 4

GROWING UP IN, WITH, AND UNDER: EVANGELISM

As Christians, we desire to see more people trust in our Savior Jesus, and so we share who He is and what He's done with those around us.

A couple years ago I had a friend who couldn't stop talking about something he discovered. It was a life-changing experience, and he wanted the world to know what he did. He must have told me about it a dozen times. I know that he told others too. He was excited to share, enthusiastic in his presentation, and prepared for all my questions.

My friend had discovered a car wash. Not just any car wash, but one where for the low price of $12 a month you could receive unlimited washes. My friend thought this was great. He couldn't believe he was just learning about it when he did. How had he lived his entire life not knowing this existed? He had experienced something he thought was valuable, and now he wanted others to experience it too.

While most of us don't get that excited over a car wash, all of us have experienced things we can't wait to share. When we discover something that has changed our life, you want others to be changed too. I know I have been an evangelist for our national parks, for certain brands of laptops and phones, and for my favorite restaurants because of how much I've enjoyed them. And if we are excited evangelists for consumer products or entertainment venues, how much more should we be willing sharers of the Gospel of Jesus Christ.

━━

The Good News of Jesus is deeply personal. The love of Christ is not an abstract thought or just a nice idea. No, Jesus gave up His life out of love for you. Yes, you. When He stretched out His arms on the cross, he was welcoming you into eternity. His resurrection from the grave brings you life everlasting.

God knows you and loves you deeply, personally, and intimately.

The Gospel is for you, but not just for you. John 3:16 reminds us that "For God so loved the world." Jesus' love is both personal and universal, which means that He wants everyone to experience and trust what we have experienced and trusted in. And, He wants to work through us to make that happen.

If you don't believe me, just read the book of Acts. One of the most memorable stories from Acts is the story of Saul who God called and renamed Paul. If you remember the story, one day a man named Saul is heading down the road to a place called Damascus when Jesus shows up. A light shined down from Heaven, Jesus called out to Him, and Saul's life was forever changed. It's an amazing story, but Saul's conversion is out of the ordinary. That's not how God usually works. Most of us don't have a Damascus Road experience where God speaks to us with a flash of light. Instead, God calls most of us through other people: parents, teachers, pastors, or friends.

The book of Acts is full of people that God used to share the Gospel. Of course, there are the well-known people like Paul and Peter, Philip and Stephen, or Barnabas and Timothy. But, there is also Lydia, Priscilla, and Aquila. God worked through each of them to extend His Kingdom and make known His name and work. In just a few decades the message of Jesus traveled across the world. And, it wasn't because these people were so great or because of their strong faith. It was because of their great and strong God who is able to work even through broken, imperfect people like you and me.

Paul's story reminds us that God can use anyone. After God showed up in Paul's life in that amazing way, God used him to share the Gospel around the world. But, before that Damascus Road event Paul had been a vigilant enemy of Jesus. Paul had been hunting down Christians to put them to death. Acts chapter 7 tells us the story of a faithful man named Stephen who was killed for his faith by the religious leaders, and we know that Paul was there that day, overseeing the atrocity. Paul's story is a reminder that God can work through anyone and everyone to spread His love.

Paul understood this deeply. In Ephesians chapter 3 Paul writes: "This grace was given to me—the least of all the saints—to proclaim to the Gentiles the incalculable riches of Christ" (3:8). "The least of all the saints" was used by God, but he wasn't alone. Paul goes on to write just a verse later that "God's multi-faceted wisdom may now be made known through the church" (3:10). For some reason, in God's infinite wisdom He has chosen to work through His children: the Church. We might wish he had chosen another way, but there is no avoiding it. God works through His people. That includes you!

———

When I was in college I worked part-time at a coffee shop. I loved the job. What I liked most about it was how many people I got to meet. Police officers, firefighters, teachers, bankers, business owners, and families would all make their way into the shop. It was fun to hear their stories, learn about their jobs, and watch kids grow up over the five years I was there. I looked forward to seeing my customers each day.

Well, at least most of them. Some were a little harder to serve than others. One man in particular made life very difficult for us. Carl was a complainer. He complained about the coffee. He complained about his wife and kids. He complained about the government and the president. Carl was just not an optimistic person. When I saw him walking down the street, making his way to the coffee shop, I would try to get his drink ready as quickly as I could so that he would be out the door as soon as possible.

One day, after a particularly rough interaction with Carl, I remember complaining about him to another coworker. "I can't stand him," I said. "I wish he would find somewhere else to go. Why does he always have to complain? He's the kind of customer I dread."

I was expecting my coworker, and good friend, to pile on. I thought that he must be thinking the same thing as me. But, his reaction was surprising. He paused. Smiled. And then said, "I love customers like Carl. I look at Carl and see someone that God loves— he just doesn't know it yet. I've actually been trying to find ways to share Jesus with Carl. I know his life would be so different."

I didn't know what to say to that. My coworker was 100 percent right. I had viewed Carl as an obstacle and something to be avoided rather than as a child of God. I looked at him and saw a nuisance, but God looked at him and saw someone He wanted to save and redeem. And while it would have been easier to just pour Carl's coffee and move onto the next customer, maybe God had placed him in my life because He wanted me to learn something—God wants to use me to share what I have.

Maybe you don't feel ready. Or, maybe you don't think you know enough or are eloquent enough to share your faith. The thought of "evangelism" or sharing the Good News of Jesus can be scary. Most of us don't feel prepared. But, as you consider the call to reflect God's love to the world consider these four things.

First, all of us need to continue to grow and learn. If you don't feel like you have it all figured out when it comes to your faith (and none of us do!), continue to dig into your Bible, attend worship and Bible study, and learn from more mature Christians. Keep on studying and growing in God's Word.

Second, remember that the Gospel is not a list of facts you need to memorize, but a story of God's loving work in the world. Everyone likes a good story, and evangelism is nothing more than sharing God's story. If you've ever heard or recited the Apostles' Creed, then you have heard all you need to know and share. While memorizing Bible facts and verses is often helpful, no one is ever converted through facts and figures. Also, don't be afraid to say, "I'm not sure. Let me think more about that." Then dive back into God's Word. Keep on listening to the story. The more you hear it and absorb it, the more you will be able to share God's story of creation and salvation.

Third, never forget that evangelism is God's work. He is in control. No one will ever get to Heaven's gates only to hear from God, "Well, I would love to let you in, but your friend [fill in your name] messed up and didn't get the job done. Sorry!" Creating and sustaining faith is all up to God. Yes, He works through you, but it's His work from start to finish. On those days when you feel like you've really messed up or missed out on an opportunity, trust that God has got it all. Rest easy in His grace and love.

Finally, keep in mind that you don't need to travel to a foreign country or quit your day job. The best evangelism takes place right where you are. The everyday places God has called us to (our workplaces, our homes, our neighborhoods, our gyms, and our coffee shops) are the very places God wants us to share our faith. As you teach your kids the faith, as you comfort a grieving neighbor, and as you encourage a friend with Jesus, you are sharing the love of God. You are an evangelist!

It's tempting to leave evangelism to the so-called

experts such as pastors, preachers, or missionaries. After all, they have the training and the gifts. But, maturity doesn't say, "I don't have to share my faith, because someone else will." Instead, maturity says, "I have received the most amazing, eternal gift I could ever imagine. I have been forgiven. I am loved. I have a God who gave everything to call me His child. This is a gift I need to share!" As mature Christians, we look for opportunities to share what we have, we challenge one another to break out of our comfort zones, and at the end of the day we rest easy in the God who is in control. Sharing our faith is part of growing up in, with, and under Jesus.

HEALTHY HABITS FOR MATURE CHRISTIANS: EVANGELISM

1. Write out the Gospel message in your own words. Before you can share your faith in Jesus, it's important to be able to articulate it yourself.

2.Share the Gospel with someone you know and trust as practice. Ask for feedback.

3.Pray for the people in your life who don't know Jesus. Ask for Christ to turn their hearts and minds and reveal His goodness.

4.Pray for God to give you open doors to share the Gospel, and for the strength to walk through those doors.

5. Memorize the Apostles' Creed (a simple, concise summary of the story of our faith) and a few of your favorite Bible passages that have been a blessing to you. Be willing to share these beloved passages just like you'd be willing to share a favorite restaurant recommendation.

CHAPTER 5

GROWING UP IN, WITH, AND UNDER: DAILY HOLINESS

As Christians, we strive to live lives that are devoted to God, reflect His Holiness, and follow His good and gracious will.

When you think of a totally devoted follower of Jesus— a true disciple—what words come to mind? How would you describe that person? When I answered that question, I thought of words like *extraordinary, radical, zealous,* and *special.*

To be sure, the Christian life is extraordinary. It does call us to be radical in some regards. I would like to think of it as special too. But, listen to how Paul describes it in 1 Thessalonians 4:11-12: "seek to lead a quiet life, to mind your own business, and to work with your own hands, as we commanded you, so that you may behave properly in the presence of outsiders and not be dependent on anyone."

That sounds very normal and ordinary to me. We aren't called to be superwomen or supermen. We don't need to set the world on fire or gather a following of thousands. What we *are* called to be is holy.

Try telling that to your friends, though! Can you imagine the reactions you might get if you let your friends and family know that you are striving toward holiness? Ha! You might get some funny looks. You might hear things like, "Good luck with that!" or "So, do you think you're better than us now?" or "That's fine for you, but I'd rather have some fun!" But, God makes it clear—we are supposed to live holy lives. He puts it bluntly in 1 Thessalonians 4:7, "For God has not called us to impurity but to live in holiness." Your daily life as a Christian is to be a holy life: a life that is dedicated to God. The Christian life is one that is "set apart" for a special purpose. Your life is not your own to do what you want with. You belong to God, and you follow His ways now, not the ways of the world. By living a holy life, you are reflecting the love of Jesus to the world. Through your holy thoughts, words, and actions the world gets a glimpse of Jesus.

———

In order to live a holy life you do not need to run away to live in a monastery. It doesn't mean you need to move to Africa and become a missionary. It certainly doesn't mean that you are better than anyone else, more worthy of God's love, or that you are perfect or better than anyone else. Living a holy life is not one we live with our chests puffed out, chins up, and pinkies out.

To put it simply, a holy life is one lived in love for God and in loving service to our neighbors. It's not a puzzle you need to put together or a mystical mystery that needs to be solved. God has graciously laid out the way to holy living in the Ten Commandments. You can (and should!) read through all of them in Exodus 20:1-17, but Jesus summarizes them in Matthew 22:37-40 when He says, "Love the Lord your God with all your heart, with all your soul, and with all your mind. This is the greatest and most important command. The second is like it: Love your neighbor as yourself. All the Law and the Prophets depend on these two commands."

Mature Christians are constantly striving to live out those two commands wherever, whenever, and with whomever God has placed us. Again, we don't need to hide away in a monastery to live holy lives, and we don't have to move to a faraway mission field. God has placed each of us in particular places, among particular people (our friends, coworkers, neighbors, and families), at particular times, where we can love in real, tangible ways. He has given us parents and other authorities to respect and honor, neighbors we can help and support, friends we can encourage and build up, and coworkers we can speak the truth in love to.

Living holy lives doesn't mean that we are better than anyone else. It's just what God's children do as we try our best to live like our Father. It's how we reflect who He is to the world. And, in fact, the longer we are leading these holy lives, the more we will see all the ways we fall short! Eventually, if we are honest with ourselves, we will see that we aren't on some gradually upward climb to perfection. No, we are just broken sinners in need of a Savior like everyone else. But, we don't despair. Instead we cling that much tighter to our Savior Jesus.

God has rules and commands for us—there is no way around it. These rules show us what a holy life looks like. While most of us love to talk about the love of God and His unending grace for all people, we might not like to focus too much on the rules. Rules feel restrictive, and we want to be free.

But, the truth is that true freedom is only found when there are boundaries.

Think about it this way: imagine a train heading down the tracks at 60 mph. If the tracks were to suddenly disappear, there would be disaster. Trains don't go very far (or at all) if there are no tracks to guide them forward. The tracks give the train the freedom to move forwards or backwards, to go fast or slow, and to travel to any number of cities and destinations. God's rules and commands are like railroad tracks. With them there is movement and growth and you can push forward. Without them you can't move at all. You stagnate, and you're trapped.

Or think about any classroom you've ever been in. There is freedom within the classroom rules. Take away the rules, and chaos reigns. Chaos is much more restrictive than it is freeing. The rules allow for freedom. Within the boundaries of those rules you can do whatever you want. That's true freedom. As much as we might like to think that we would be okay in a world without commands, that we don't need them, or that we are held back by God's stuffy, old-fashioned rules, we need them more than we know and in them we are free. A life lived within the walls of God's will is a life of true freedom.

And so, as God's children, we delight in His commands. We recognize that far from holding us back, they actually allow us to grow. We do our best to follow His commands because we know that they are good for us. We trust that in giving us these rules that God has our best interests in mind.

———

When I picture someone living a holy life, I think of Brad. Brad is a member of one of my former churches. He is a simple man with a simple faith. He isn't college educated. He has never gone on a mission trip. He doesn't lead a Bible study. No one is wowed by his eloquent prayers and beautiful sermons. But, Brad believes in Jesus. He trusts in his Savior. Brad knows that he is loved.

And Brad reflects that love to others. Each Sunday Brad was the first one at church. I would often get to church early to go over my sermon and pray for our worship, but Brad would always beat me there. He would unlock the doors, make sure everything was in place, and light the candles for worship. And then he would sit down to spend some time with his Christian brothers before worship began. Week after week Brad did all this. I was probably one of the few who noticed. He never won any awards for his service. It wasn't the kind of work that got the attention of anyone important. But, that's not why he did it. Brad just loved His Lord and wanted to serve His people. And that is holy living.

━━

While we strive towards holiness, the reality is we will never reach it. The road of holy living is one marked by failures and falls. That's where repentance comes in. In Mark's Gospel, Jesus' first words are "The time is fulfilled, and the kingdom of God has come near. Repent and believe the good news!" A crucial aspect of holy living is repentance.

Repentance, literally, means to turn. To repent is to turn away from your sins, mistakes, and failings and to turn toward God's grace and mercy. To repent is to say "sorry," but it goes far deeper than that. Repentance requires genuine regret for what you've done, but it also includes believing in God's forgiveness through Jesus.

None of us is perfect. All of us have sinned. And, by the power of the Holy Spirit, God calls us to a lifetime of repentance. It's not something we do only in worship on Sunday. It's a daily, hourly turning. It's admitting that our problem called sin is far greater than we ever imagined, but also that God's grace goes deeper than we deserve. Living a holy life isn't about "having it all together." While we are striving to "be perfect, therefore, as your heavenly Father is perfect" (Matthew 5:48), we continually repent. We turn away from sin and toward God's open arms of love.

Mature Christians are always striving toward daily holy living. We want to keep God's commands, and we sincerely thank Him for giving them to us. The beauty in Christian holiness is that it often looks very normal and ordinary. It looks like moms and dads loving their kids with the love of Christ. It looks like business-people working hard and honestly. It looks like neighbors acting like neighbors instead of strangers. Christian maturity looks like average people doing average things, but for very un-average reasons: out of love for God and in loving service to the people around us. By living holy lives, we are reflecting God's holiness to the world and letting everyone we know what kind of God we have.

Christian maturity doesn't say, "Why would I follow the rules if God will just forgive me?" Christian maturity says, "I have been loved and forgiven more than I deserve, and so I want to reflect that love in my actions to the world."

Christian maturity doesn't say, "No one is going to tell me what to do—I want to be free!" but rejoices in the true freedom found within the boundaries of God's will. Christian maturity recognizes that holy living doesn't earn us anything, but is a response to what Christ earned for us on the cross. By living holy lives, we grow up in, with, and under Jesus.

HEALTHY HABITS FOR MATURE CHRISTIANS: DAILY HOLINESS

1. Review the 10 Commandments. Evaluate your life in light of them. Where have you fallen short? What changes do you need to make? What attitudes and actions need to be adjusted? What sin needs to be repented of?

2.Find a Christian friend or mentor who can encourage and challenge you to live like Christ. Share your struggles, admit your mistakes, and be open to correction.

3.Pray for the Holy Spirit to mold you into Christ's image and strengthen you to live like Jesus.

4.Write out a list of opportunities God has placed in

front of you to share His love. Who has God placed in your life that you can serve? In what ways can you share His love in your daily life?

5.Develop a habit of repentance. None of us is perfect. When you have fallen short and haven't lived a holy life, confess your sins to those you have hurt, to God, and even to a pastor (who is there to represent God to you). Rather than brushing our sins under a rug and pretending they "aren't that bad," admit the depth of your problem. And then, hear God's Word of forgiveness. Trust that His grace is for you. Believe that His cross-shaped love washes away your sin.

CHAPTER 6

GROWING UP IN, WITH, AND UNDER: JESUS

As Christians, we believe and trust that Jesus is our only hope, our source of life, and the provider of our eternal rest.

A couple years ago I was sitting at a coffee shop getting some work done when I noticed a man sitting across from me reading the newspaper. His words were stumbling. His accent was thick. He struggled to put together the sentences he was reading aloud. As I listened, it became clear that English was not his first language. I wondered if he even understood what he was reading.

What I came to realize was that he was trying to

learn the language. The words he was reading were probably just sounds and jumbled letters to him. But, over time, with practice and repetition, those letters would turn into words. If he could just stick with it, those words would come together into sentences. And eventually those sentences would form ideas and stories. One day, he would learn the language.

And to me, that's what it's like to grow up in, with, and under Jesus. When we first begin this journey, much of it might not make sense. We'll go to church and be confused by what's going on. Our prayers will be short and awkward. When we read the Bible, the stories will sound strange. Sharing our faith will seem overwhelming. We won't act very Christian most of the time.

But, over time, by the power of the Holy Spirit, under the guidance of God's Word, and filled with the grace of Jesus, things will change. We will mature. The language of God's Word will make sense to us. We won't learn it all at once, but God will work in us to mold us in His image.

If we were to track our maturity over time on a graph, I don't think we'd see a gradually rising line pointing upwards. There would be some moments of upwards climbing, some moments of peaks. But, there would also be a lot of valleys.

It's not as though once we are set on this path of discipleship by Jesus that we slowly and surely figure it out until we reach the destination of Christian perfection. We might have seasons where we grow and mature quickly, where true progress is made by the power of the Holy Spirit. And then there will be the seasons of life when we are so far off the map we don't know how to make it back on track.

And that can be frustrating. It can be hard when we honestly reflect on our lives to see where we've fallen short and failed. We might even get angry at ourselves for the ways we've abandoned our walks with Christ and gone our own way. But, Christian maturity isn't about figuring it out. It's not about reaching perfection. It's about trusting in Jesus.

As we continue to grow up, we will see more and more that we can't, but Jesus can. We will see that we've failed over and over again—but Jesus is victorious. We will see that we are weak—but He is strong. We'll realize that while we've fallen too many times to count, Jesus stands firm. Of course, we don't celebrate our failings and sins, but we let them drive us to the cross of Jesus Christ. They remind us just how much we need our savior. The more we grow up, the more we see how much we need a Savior. And over time we will see that Jesus is exactly the Savior we need.

I pray that as you spend time in God's Word you will see Jesus more and more. I hope that as you surround yourself with your brothers and sisters and worship your glorious king you will come to trust in your Savior. It's my desire that as you pray, as you share your faith, and as you strive toward holy living, that all of that will point you more toward the cross. That's Christian maturity. That's growing up in, with, and under Jesus.

THANK YOU!

If you enjoyed this book or received value from it in any way, then I'd like to ask you for a favor: would you be kind enough to leave a review for this book on Amazon? It'd be greatly appreciated!

ABOUT THE AUTHOR

Peter Berauer was born and raised in the suburbs of Chicago, where he currently lives and serves as a pastor.

Peter married his high school sweetheart who continues to amaze him everyday.

When Peter isn't at church he is probably either running or drinking coffee

For more information visit: www.pwilliamb.com

 facebook.com/pberauer

 instagram.com/pwberauer

Made in the USA
Columbia, SC
30 May 2019